NORTHWEST COAST INDIANS
Coloring Book

by
David
Rickman

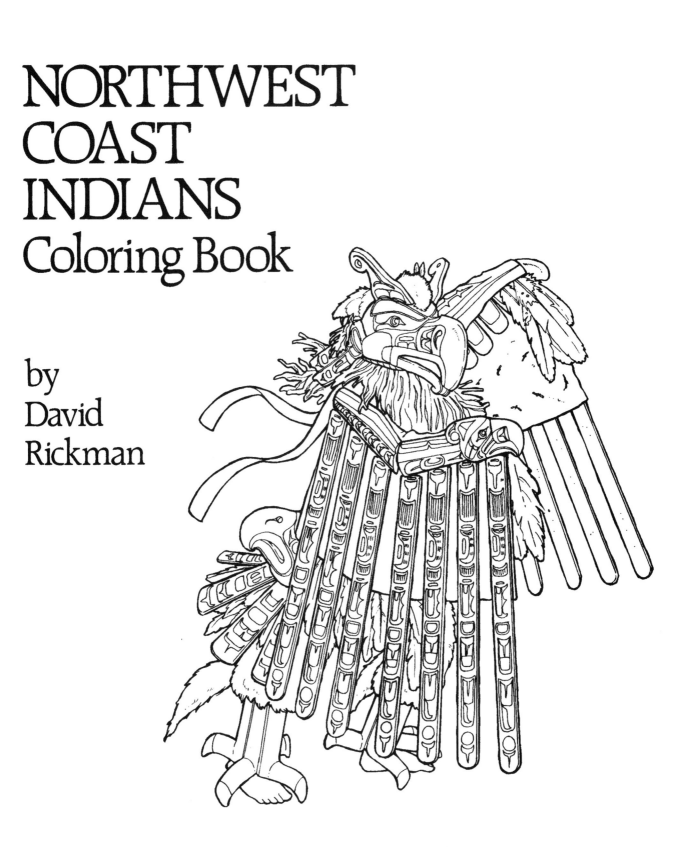

Dover Publications, Inc., New York

For my father and mother

Northwest Coast Indians Coloring Book is a new work, first
published by Dover Publications, Inc. in 1984.

DOVER *Pictorial Archive* SERIES

This book belongs to the Dover Pictorial Archive Series.
You may use the designs and illustrations for graphics
and crafts applications, free and without special
permission, provided that you include no more than four
in the same publication or project. (For permission for
additional use, please write to Dover Publications, Inc.,
31 East 2nd Street, Mineola, N.Y. 11501.)
    However, republication or reproduction of any
illustration by any other graphic service whether it be in
a book or in any other design resource is strictly
prohibited.

International Standard Book Number: 0-486-24728-7

Manufactured in the United States of America
Dover Publications, Inc., 31 East 2nd Street, Mineola,
N.Y. 11501

Introduction

The Northwest Coast: the land plunges steeply to the ocean, gray fogs cling to dark forests and the sky echoes to the crashing of waves. This is the realm of the killer whale and raven, of the Salmon Men and the thunderbird. Once wooden villages that clung to the shore sheltered a hardy and independent people whose way of life depended entirely on the forest and the sea. Warming waters from the Japan Current wash the coast of this narrow strip of land that reaches from southern Alaska down to northern California. Game animals and fish flourish in the mild climate, and so, in the midst of abundance, did the people.

Here civilizations were created that honored wealth and rank won through strength, competition, courage and generosity. But a strict caste system also prevailed, with "noble" or "commoner" status depending on birth and wealth. Families of the highborn struggled to keep themselves at the top of the social order through strategic marriages, the careful accumulation of fortunes and the creation of obligations by dispensing those fortunes to the public. One measure of wealth was the possession of slaves, who stood at the bottom of the social scale. As war captives, debtors or the children of slaves, they had no status and were often destroyed with other property in calculated displays of prosperity.

It is easy to make these peoples sound too similar to one another, although there were many languages, beliefs and customs in this vast land. Yet some generalizations ring true. Like all Native Americans, the people of the Northwest Coast were certain to involve their religions in virtually every phase of their lives. Tales of the creation, lessons taught by the spirits to deserving human beings and stories of their willingness to assist in heroic undertakings were repeated often, especially to children. Much of the wealth held by important families went toward staging dazzling ceremonies to honor the higher powers. Direct communication between humans and spirits, however, was generally performed by shamans, men or women with special gifts as well as training in so dangerous a task. Shamans, whether they used their powers for good or ill, were regarded throughout the Northwest Coast with both awe and fear.

A person's relationship to the environment is another area in which it is possible to generalize. Water dominated the lives of all these peoples, whether they lived near ocean or stream. In this rugged terrain, travel, even for short distances, was by canoe. With paddle in hand, the people of the Northwest Coast journeyed for trade, hunting and fishing, and went to war. These were a people at home on the water—even small children confidently managed canoes.

Conversely, they felt a strong distrust of the inland reaches. Every village was backed by dense forest that forever seemed ready to overwhelm the houses. The deep woodlands were a place of wonder and mystery where only brave souls ventured to hunt and gather supplies.

Wood was the most important supply taken from the forests. The lives of the Northwest Coast peoples depended on wood. Their craftspeople fashioned it by carving, bending and weaving it into everything from fishhooks to clothing. A piece of wood, when sensitively carved and painted, could become a profound piece of fine art in the form of a religious mask or a memorial pole.

The genius of the art of the Northwest Coast is striking. With its emphasis on geometric and animal forms, rich combinations of wood, shell, bone and fur, its brilliant colors and graceful design, this distinctive art may be the best-loved gift these peoples have left to us. It was, in fact, probably the only aspect of native life that early visitors to the coast found admirable.

As it did everywhere else on the continent, the downfall of the native cultures on the Northwest Coast began with the arrival of the white man. Russians, English, French, Spanish and Americans began coming in the eighteenth century in search of valuable furs. With one hand they offered unheard-of wealth in trade goods, and with the other they brought sure destruction through disease, corruption, suppression of ancient religions and removal of local resources.

Despite incredible obstacles, some of these peoples have begun to revive. Renewed pride in themselves is seen everywhere, from the rediscovery of ancient languages and religions to a renaissance of the arts. Once again a hardy and independent people thrives on the Northwest Coast.

In preparing this book I have become indebted to many, including the numerous explorers and scholars, alive and dead, who have attempted to understand a culture not their own and to preserve a part of it. I wish I could thank them all. I do, however, wish to thank my wife, Helen K. Davie, an illustrator in her own right, for her lovingly offered advice and encouragement.

1. Nootka, late eighteenth century. The peoples of the Northwest Coast were competitive in almost every area: wealth, status, territory and war. Many were headhunters whose predawn attacks on villages caught their victims asleep and defenseless. The Nootka of Vancouver Island were dreaded warriors. We see here a war chief painted red and black for war, wearing a cedar-bark corselet and carrying stone and bone clubs. Though most men went into battle naked, he wears a cedar-bark loincloth and a bearskin cloak. The carved wooden head resembles the trophies of war, but probably served a more symbolic purpose.

2. Makah, late eighteenth to early nineteenth centuries. The Makah, with the related Nootka and Quileute, were the only true whale hunters of the Northwest Coast. Other tribes were content to wait for the occasional beached whale, but the people of western Vancouver Island and the Olympic Peninsula would launch expeditions of up to ten canoes, carrying whalers who had trained and prayed for success. Whales were struck from as close as three feet, after which a wounded whale might tow the sealskin floats and the canoe out to sea for days. The whale's meat and oil were divided up among the entire village.

3. Kwakiutl, late eighteenth century. The early European visitors found these natives of northern Vancouver Island dressed in costumes well suited to the climate. Like most peoples of the Northwest Coast, the Kwakiutl wore little or no clothing when the weather was mild. Otherwise, garments of woven cedar bark trimmed with fur were worn. Head deformation was considered a mark of beauty and high status, as were the ornaments of copper and shell.

4. Tlingit, late eighteenth century. One of the most populous and powerful peoples on the Northwest Coast, the Tlingit of southern Alaska impressed the early explorers. Here a highborn woman and her husband stand before funeral monuments that contain the ashes of their ancestors. Wide-brimmed rain hats, full beards, wooden lip-plugs and shell nose-ornaments were common to many of these peoples, but struck the newcomers as unlike the costumes of any other Native Americans they had ever seen.

5. Klallam, 1825. The peoples of the Northwest Coast were weavers. Among the Salish of the Strait of Georgia this art produced robes of exceptional beauty. The women combined plant fibers with the wool of mountain goats and other furs and drew them out on a unique form of spindle to create their yarns. Blankets were highly prized and traded widely through the Northwest. The older woman wears the traditional clothing of the Salish, while the younger woman with the partially completed basket wears a new style made from trade cloth. Both have their arms and legs tattooed.

6. Chinook, 1832. These once-proud merchant lords of the Columbia River controlled the trade in furs with visiting sea captains, and were the "Flatheads" who met the Lewis and Clark expedition. Yet by the 1830s the Chinook were a devastated people. Overhunting, alcohol and finally disease, which took nine out of ten people, resulted from the coming of "civilization" to the coast. Here is a wealthy elderly couple with their grandchild on a cradleboard that will shape the child's head. Behind them stand the graves of their people.

7. Nootka, 1778. Homes on the Northwest Coast, crafted of split logs, were large enough for extended families to live in. The floors were of earth and there were benches and mats surrounding the central cooking fire. Personal possessions were stored neatly in boxes of steamed and bent wood. The large wooden statues were family emblems. Long-term food supplies (dried

fish) hung conveniently from the rafters. For cooking, water could be boiled in wooden boxes by adding heated stones. The Nootka's clothing consisted of three basic garments: an oblong robe of cedar bark that could be worn as a cloak, a skirt or a toga; a triangular rain cape; and a conical woven hat.

8. Karok, 1851. The most southerly peoples who could be called "Northwest Coast" lived in Northern California. Here the strictly upheld class system, the emphasis on wealth and the dependence on water for food and transportation still prevailed. The Karok and their neighbors were skilled artisans, whose firmly woven baskets could hold even boiling water. This woman is also carrying a carved porridge stirrer. Her clothing is very typical of the area: basket-cap, tattooed chin and arm, and a double-apron skirt of painted hide and braided grass ornamented with shells.

9. Quinault, mid-nineteenth century. As with all the peoples of the Northwest Coast, most of the Quinault's food came from fish taken in a wide variety of ways. Salmon, the most favored fish, were caught on their spawning runs up the Washington coast rivers in wooden weirs. These were barriers across calmer rivers where men could dip out the fish with huge nets. Salmon could also be speared in the shallows with two-pronged harpoons with detachable points. This was often the work of older men, no longer able to lift the heavy nets.

10. Comox, mid-nineteenth century. Living on the Gulf of Georgia that lies between Vancouver Island and the Canadian coast, the Comox spoke the Salish language. Their land, in common with the rest of the Northwest Coast, was a wet one. The warming Japan Current also brought rain and fog. Clothing made of plant fibers was designed to shed water. In addition, the man is wearing a fur vest for warmth and moccasins (which were only worn for long journeys). His wife is carrying a berry-filled basket suspended from her head by a tumpline.

11. Yurok, 1852. War was not as frequent among the Californian peoples as it was at the northern end of the coast. Yet, when fought, it was serious enough. War parties traveled by canoe to the enemy village and struck, when possible, without warning. In common with peoples throughout the Northwest Coast, the Yurok built houses of wood and skillfully hollowed out canoes from single logs. Their clothing, too, had close parallels throughout this region.

12. Tlingit, late eighteenth to early nineteenth centuries. Armored and emblazoned with heraldic crests, the Tlingit warriors in many ways resembled European knights. A rigorous training from youth and a strict code of honor bound each man. Important warriors wore heavy wooden helmets and face masks, twined wooden corselets over hide tunics and a heavy collection of weapons, including copper or iron short swords. They were the terror of their enemies, including the Russians, with whom they fought for control of Alaska. Firearms, quickly adopted by the Tlingit, relegated armor to the status of ceremonial costume.

13. Cowichan, 1840. It was reported by early visitors that Salish weavers, the Cowichan included, used the fur of specially bred white dogs in weaving their robes. How true this is is not certain, for mountain-goat hair seems to have been the most important ingredient. The white and multicolored robes that resulted were exceptionally valuable and were considered fit wear for a chief. This chief is wearing a medicine cap of human hair and feathers.

14. California–Oregon border, 1850. Warriors throughout this region had a similar style of dress. Most went to war naked or in loincloths, but important men were protected with twined wooden corselets or a tunic of folded elk hide. On the head a thick cap of panther or elk hide was worn. Otherwise the hair was bound up and sharp spikes were run through the knot to prevent it from being grabbed.

15. Kwakiutl, late nineteenth century. Elaborate ceremonials were staged during the long, cold months of winter. Of the secret societies that organized and performed these rituals, one, the Hamatsas, created the most spectacular. Annually they initiated the men and women who wished to become shamans into the society. The ritual was brilliantly presented in a dimly lit house where novices, possessed by the cannibal spirit, leaped, screamed and bit until pacified by special rites. Masked and costumed dancers impersonated the spirits who participated. Some of the masks were made to spring open to reveal a second face below. Others had workable jaws that snapped when the spirit gave its cry.

16. Tlingit, 1818. The foreign influence on native clothing in the Northwest was already being seen by the early nineteenth century. Mass-produced cloth for women's dresses and men's shirts was one of the first intrusions. Yet many traditional garments of symbolic purpose persisted. The hat of woven spruce root with copper rings indicates that this man is a clan leader who has given many potlatches (ceremonial feasts). His woven robe is similar to those made by the Salish. A fringed dance apron and Athabaskan trousers are important, because in this wet climate leather was worn as a luxury only. He wears a Russian peace medal around his neck. Ravens were sacred on the Northwest Coast, and so were usually left undisturbed.

17. Coast Salish, mid-nineteenth century. The working dress of most men on the British Columbian coast was similar. At most, it was a front apron of hide or bark that could be tucked through the legs and into the back of the belt when the wearer was busy. Usually it was not even this. For warmth, a cloak or vest of fur was added. Throughout this region, the heads of the freeborn were intentionally deformed. These men are working with stone and bone tools to shape their sleek, sturdy canoes.

18. Tolowa, 1855. Originally the Tolowa dressed much like their neighbors, the Yurok and the Karok. Yet by the mid-nineteenth century European clothing and goods were common and eagerly sought. This change of appearance was superficial, but it was an omen of the deeper erosion of environment and culture that would take place in generations to come.

19. Tsimshian, 1850. Eagle down was the symbol of holy spirits to the Northwest Coast Indians. The Tsimshian, who lived on the coast of British Columbia, piled it atop their headdresses so that it drifted out when they danced. Most of the neighboring peoples did the same. This man stands before a carved and painted crest screen that symbolizes his family. His woven cloak, shell-inlaid headdress with an ermine train and walrus-whisker crest, his shell nose-ring and his raven rattle are all signs of wealth and high rank.

20. Olympic Peninsula, 1862. This couple of the Quileute or Makah were related to the Nootka of Vancouver Island. They were whalers and fishermen who braved the open ocean in thirty-foot canoes. The man wears a bearskin cloak and woven hat, no longer with a distinctive knob. Both have traditional shell ornaments and tattoos. But trade goods have replaced the woman's cedar-bark garments with cloth. Men working with American fur hunters in Alaska brought back the idea of waterproof seal-gut parkas.

21. Tlingit, mid-nineteenth century. Among the peoples of the Northwest Coast, shamans occupied a powerful position. As healers, prophets and direct intermediaries with the spirit world, these women and men had great influence. The Tlingit shamans were striking people, often marked either with such physical deformities as bowlegs or crossed eyes, or else with the uncommon red hair. They were never allowed to comb or cut their hair. When communing with the spirits they usually wore only a dance apron, for mischievous spirits liked to steal their clothing. This man wears a crown of horns and a necklace of bones, as well as a fin symbolizing the killer whale.

22. Haida, 1880. The best-known symbol of the Northwest Coast is the totem pole. In fact, "totem pole" is not a proper name for these objects, since they did more than symbolize a family crest, or totem. They began as ornamented house posts, entryways for dwellings, memorials and mortuaries for the deceased. Increased wealth through trade with the white man, as well as the introduction of metal tools, led to their great elaboration and growth in popularity. Never, though, did they spread outside of the northernmost part of this region. The Haida of Queen Charlotte and Prince of Wales Islands were famous carvers of these monuments.

23. Puyallup-Nisqually, mid-nineteenth century. Horses came to this people's homeland on
Puget Sound through trade with tribes in inland Washington and Idaho. In a land blessed with so
many interconnected waterways, horses were adopted only by those who lived furthest inland.
Both the man and the woman here wear poncholike shirts of shredded cedar bark. A distinguish-
ing mark of the hunter was a cougar skin worn over the shoulder, supporting a quiver of the same
hide.

24. Skykomish, mid-nineteenth century. Autumn was a good time for hunting in the mountains near Puget Sound. Though the usual male costume there was nudity, special clothing was put on for cool weather and hard traveling. Shirts of hide with the hair still on them were worn, often with a bearskin cloak pulled over and belted at the waist. Hide leggings and moccasins protected the legs and feet. Hunters distinguished themselves by wearing the upper part of a mountain goat's head on their own.

25. Salish, late nineteenth to early twentieth centuries. Despite more than a century of foreign domination, the peoples of the Northwest Coast continued to hold their religious and social celebrations, and to lavish care on the clothing worn in them. At times these clothes remained true to their ancient origins. This Twana woman of Puget Sound wears clothing made from hand-woven blankets, which were regarded as sacred. The Cowichan man from the Gulf of Georgia wears a headdress, representing the warrior spirit, which harks back to the deformed heads and hairstyles of his ancestors. His clothing of velvet appliquéd with ribbon was inspired by Canadian Indians from further inland, whose style of ornament was derived from the French.

26. Bella Bella, 1882. An elder of his clan waits to perform a dance that will tell the story of his people. His headdress symbolizes the spirit of the killer whale, a familiar figure in the religions of the Northwest Coast. He is huddled for warmth in a blue and red blanket decorated with mother-of-pearl buttons. Beside him are a box and ladle made by steaming and bending the wood, so carefully crafted that they held water.

27. Tlingit, late nineteenth to early twentieth centuries. A brief revival of the native economies in Alaska occurred during the Gold Rush. The money earned in services to the miners was often applied to refurbishing clan heirlooms and creating new ones emblazoned with the crests of their owners. Bears, ravens, killer whales and thunderbirds were applied to virtually everything, even painted onto faces at festivals. Seen here is a clan house with its painted front and carved doorpost. Before it stand members of different families in their finest regalia.

28. Hupa, 1897. The Hupa of northwestern California, like most of their neighbors, celebrated dances intended not only to honor the spirits, but also to display their personal wealth. In early autumn came the White Deerskin Dance, where the wealth displayed included the decorated skins of unusually colored deer, especially albinos. These dance leaders carry huge blades of obsidian and wear crowns of sea-lion tusks. The woman's clothes especially show how white fashions and morals had imposed themselves on the native styles.

29. Kwakiutl, 1895. An important institution on the Northwest Coast was the potlatch, the ritual distribution of goods by the leaders of the tribe. At the potlatch thousands of dollars in goods, including blankets, food and ornaments, could be distributed to rival clans, the challenge being to match or top this show of generosity. In fact, it was the only way known of lending and borrowing capital, and then paying it back. Clothing for such important occasions was decorated with ribbons, puffin beaks, buttons and thimbles. Large plaques of copper, a prestigious symbol of wealth, were commonly given away at these celebrations.

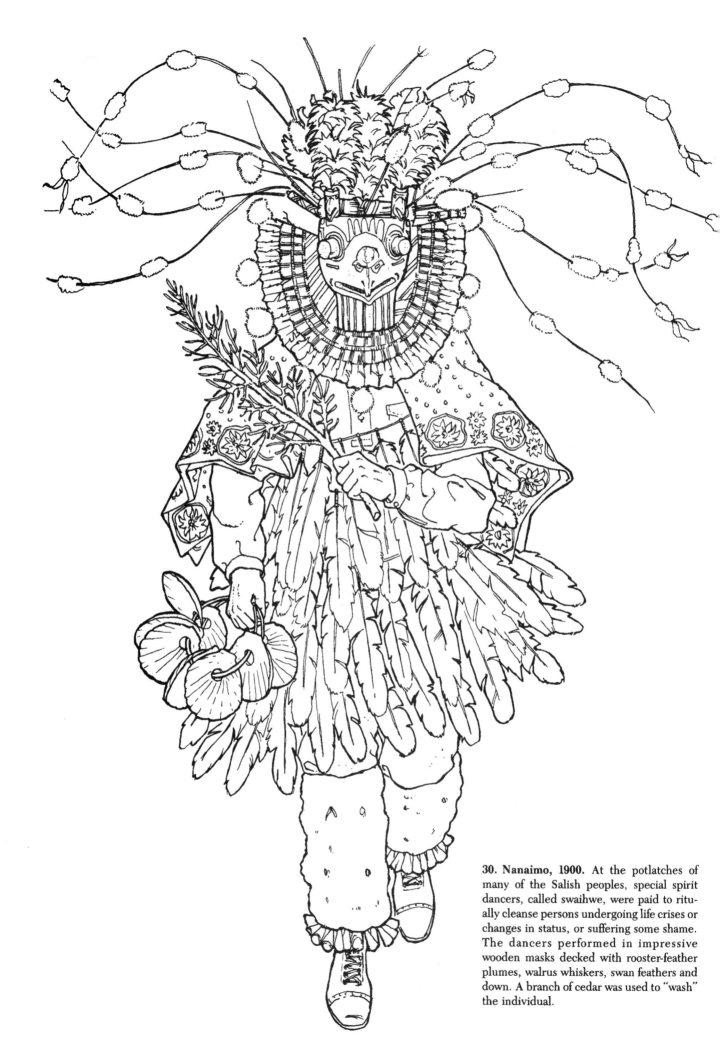

30. Nanaimo, 1900. At the potlatches of many of the Salish peoples, special spirit dancers, called swaihwe, were paid to ritually cleanse persons undergoing life crises or changes in status, or suffering some shame. The dancers performed in impressive wooden masks decked with rooster-feather plumes, walrus whiskers, swan feathers and down. A branch of cedar was used to "wash" the individual.

31. Bella Coola, 1890s. Wonderful masks were carved throughout the Northwest Coast to bring religious spirits to life. These two men from the coast of British Columbia are portraying two of the four supernatural brothers who taught their people all of the useful arts.

32. Haida, 1880s. The canoes of the Northwest Coast were carved out of single logs of wood, usually cedar, and expanded by steaming and spreading them apart. Prows and sterns were carved separately and added on. A Haida chief's "war" canoe could be up to fifty feet long and seven feet wide and could carry close to sixty people. It was propelled by paddles and was sometimes equipped with a sail. This canoe is on its way to a potlatch and will put ashore down the beach from the village so that the passengers can dress in their finest clothes and enter the harbor singing songs.

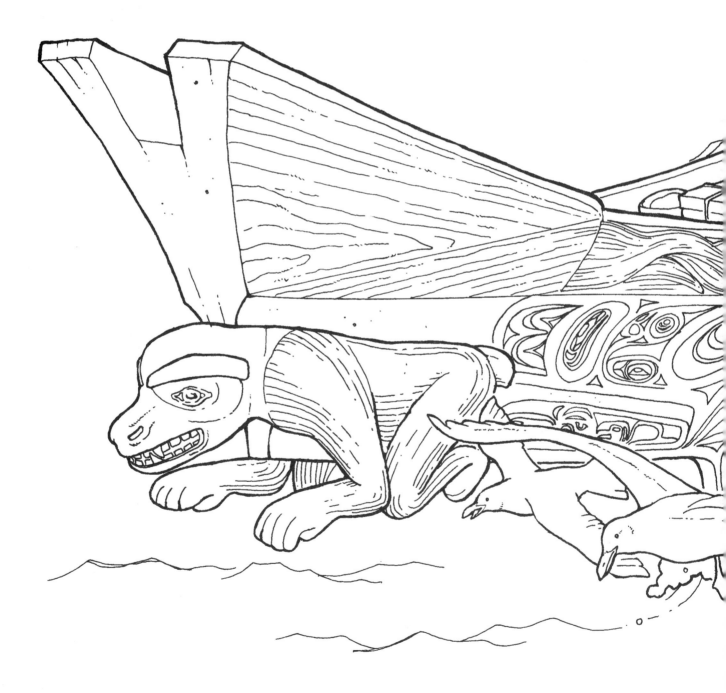

33. Kwakiutl, modern. Brilliant artistic traditions as well as ancient ceremonies are returning to many parts of the Northwest Coast. A growing pride in being a Native American has revived the arts, but ironically it is the non-Indian collector who finances the artists. This magnificent thunderbird costume, made of wood, cloth, fur, cedar bark and feathers, is now in the permanent collection of a German museum.